ENDURING MYSTERIES

AREA 51

CHRISTOPHER BAHN

CREATIVE EDUCATION • CREATIVE PAPERBACKS

Published by Creative Education and Creative Paperbacks
P.O. Box 227, Mankato, Minnesota 56002
Creative Education and Creative Paperbacks
are imprints of The Creative Company
www.thecreativecompany.us

Design by Graham Morgan
Art direction by Blue Design (www.bluedes.com)

Images by Alamy Stock Photo/Dale O'Dell , 6, Photo Researchers, 39; Getty Images/AlexTIZANO, 31, Bettmann, 22, DigitalGlobe/ScapeWare3d, 8, Jacob Wackerhausen, 35, Merlinus74, 26, Wirestock, 19; Microsoft Designer/AI Generated, cover, 1; Shutterstock/33, Alexey Stiop, 17, Claudio Divizia, 34, Everett Collection, 25, MarkauMark, 14, Photobank.kiev.ua, 44, photoBeard, 3, schmaelterphoto, 4–5, SSSCCC, 32, Steve Reed, 41, Stocksnapper, 36; SuperStock/Everett Collection, 14–15, Purestock, 20; Wikimedia Commons/Frank Pierson, 28, George Stock, 2, Henrique Alvim Corrêa , 24, Ken Lund, 12, Public Domain, 11, Public Domain/Arnold Newman , 13, Staff Sgt. Aaron Allmon II, 43, USN, 16

Every effort has been made to contact copyright holders for material reproduced in this book. Any omissions will be rectified in subsequent printings if notice is given to the publisher.

Copyright © 2025 Creative Education, Creative Paperbacks
International copyright reserved in all countries.
No part of this book may be reproduced in any form
without written permission from the publisher.

Library of Congress Cataloging-in-Publication Data
Names: Bahn, Christopher (Children's story writer), author. | Karst, Ken. Enduring mysteries.
Title: Area 51 / Christopher Bahn.
Description: Mankato, Minnesota : Creative Education and Creative Paperbacks, [2025] | Series: Enduring mysteries | Includes bibliographical references and index. | Audience: Ages 10–14 | Audience: Grades 7–9 | Summary: "An investigative approach to the mystery surrounding Area 51 for age 12 and up, from historical accounts and popular myths to hard facts and evidence. Includes a glossary, index, sidebars, and further resources"—Provided by publisher.
Identifiers: LCCN 2024015988 (print) | LCCN 2024015989 (ebook) | ISBN 9798889892847 (library binding) | ISBN 9781682776506 (paperback) | ISBN 9798889893950 (ebook)
Subjects: LCSH: Unidentified flying objects—Sightings and encounters—Nevada—Juvenile literature. | Area 51 (Nev)—Juvenile literature.
Classification: LCC TL789.2 .B34 2025 (print) | LCC TL789.2 (ebook) | DDC 001.94209793/14—dc23/eng/20240412
LC record available at https://lccn.loc.gov/2024015988
LC ebook record available at https://lccn.loc.gov/2024015989

Printed in China

CONTENTS

Introduction 9

Nothing to See Here? 10

A Manufactured Mystery 18

Little Gray Aliens 27

Watch the Skies 37

Field Notes 46

Selected Bibliography 47

Websites 47

Index 48

INTRODUCTION

OPPOSITE: An aerial view of Area 51

There is a place in the desert northwest of Las Vegas, Nevada, so mysterious that for years, the U.S. government wouldn't admit that it even existed. Its nickname is "Dreamland." But it is most well-known by a bland map designation. Some say the name was chosen to seem *deliberately* boring—to hide whatever is really going on there: Area 51.

In the 1950s, puzzling bright lights and fast-moving objects were common in the sky above this restricted military zone. People who worked there were forbidden to tell anyone what they did. Area 51 was classified as top secret until 2010 and not officially acknowledged until 2013. Why? One possible answer is: airplanes. For decades, Area 51 has been a top secret base for testing advanced new aircraft designs. It's work that must be kept quiet for reasons of national security.

But another story has taken hold. It's a wild claim that cannot be officially disproven. Some people say Area 51 hides the remains of a crashed flying saucer from outer space—perhaps even its alien pilots. The myth has spread widely in movies, books, and TV shows.

For years, military pilots have reported strange objects capable of speed and flight unknown by human science. Could Area 51 be part of a government cover-up to hide **extraterrestrial** technology?

NOTHING TO SEE HERE?

OPPOSITE: New types of spy planes were tested at Area 51 in the late 1950s.

Area 51. It sounds like a railroad yard or a spot on a game board, not a legend like Shangri-La or Atlantis. But for nearly 75 years, Area 51 has been at the center of extraordinary American stories about UFOs—unidentified flying objects.

One reason why Area 51 has spun up so many vivid tales, perhaps, has to do with the fact that nearly everything about it has been officially denied or left unexplained. This was due to the pressing need for secrecy about U.S. military projects developed at the base during the Cold War (1947–91) between the United States and the Soviet Union. *The New York Times* once described Area 51 as "a base so secret it doesn't exist." And it's a well-known **irony** that secrecy often attracts the spotlight.

But Area 51 has played a key role in American **aeronautics**, politics, and defense, even though its **budget**, operations, and employees have

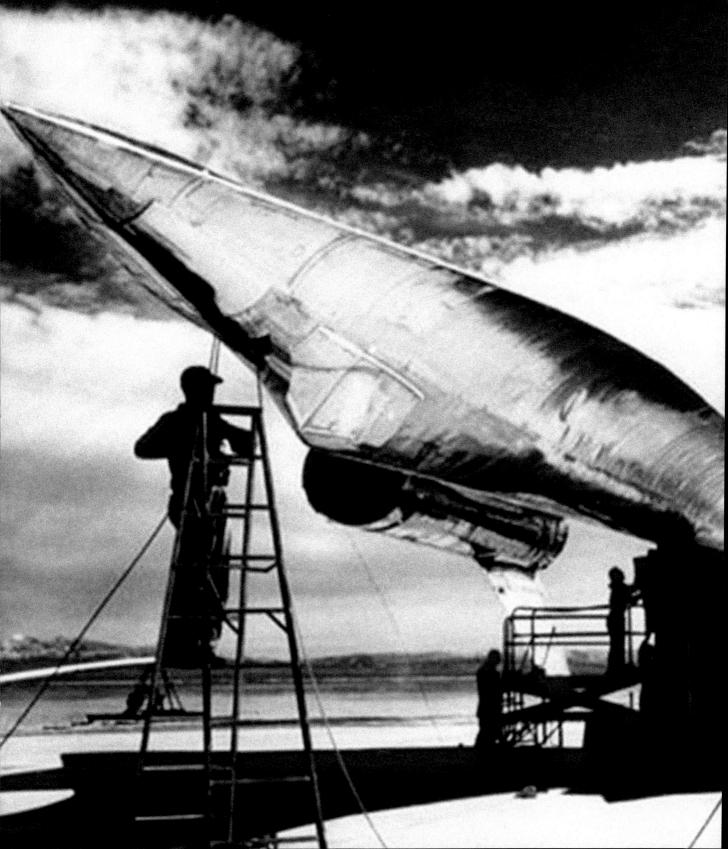

rarely been made public—sometimes not even to the president. When Lyndon Johnson took office in 1963 upon President John F. Kennedy's death, he had never heard of Area 51 or the revolutionary spy plane—the U-2—that was being developed there. But that secrecy also spawned other, more outlandish stories. For most of its existence, Area 51 has also been central to **conspiracy** theories and fringe beliefs. They involve military plots and U.S. government deception. They involve cooperation with extraterrestrial beings, secret international dealings, and fantastic technology.

It's easier to find Area 51 than it used to be. There was a time when even U.S. Geological Survey maps didn't label it. Today, the Google Maps app takes people right there. It shows runways, hangars, and other buildings—views that not long ago could have gotten a person

OPPOSITE: Groom Lake's remote location is perfect for the secretive Area 51.

PRESIDENT LYNDON JOHNSON

shot or arrested (or praised if they were a foreign spy). Area 51 is about 80 miles (129 kilometers) north of Las Vegas. It's in barren, desert terrain, an area of dry lakes and low mountains, creosote bushes and Joshua trees. It is located on a dry lakebed called Groom Lake. The Nevada Test and Training Range (NTTR), a piece of the Nevada desert as big as the state of Connecticut, surrounds it. Area 51 also abuts the U.S. Department of Energy's Nevada National Security Site, a 1,360-square-mile (3,500-sq-km) area where nearly 1,000 nuclear weapons were tested from the 1950s through the 1990s. Area 51 itself covers about 600 square miles (1,554 sq km) and is protected by heavy security both on and above the ground. Even Air Force pilots from the training range are forbidden from flying above Area 51. On the ground, security cameras and motion detectors ring the site. Hikers encounter signs telling them that the use of deadly force is authorized to keep them out. Trespassers are often quickly met by security guards in Jeeps. No one knows who employs the guards, who wear camouflage and thus are known casually as "camo dudes."

NOTHING TO SEE HERE?

No one is sure where the name "Area 51" comes from. Aviation expert Peter Merlin suggests it derives from "Project 51," a designation created by the construction company that the U.S. government hired to build the site. Over the years, officials and pilots have called it "Watertown,"

13

RIGHT: President Dwight D. Eisenhower

"Paradise Ranch," and "The Box." "Dreamland" was Area 51's official air-traffic call sign.

Why put an important military operation in the middle of nowhere? In the 1930s, that part of Nevada was wild desert, far from towns or people. In the 1950s, President Dwight D. Eisenhower ordered the development of a plane that could fly high over the Soviet Union to look at military bases, and a top secret site was needed. The project director, Richard Bissell, a professor who was a top advisor to the director of the Central **Intelligence** Agency (CIA), found Nevada's Groom Lake. It was a salt flat that was as smooth and hard as a runway and also neighbored the NTTR. The site was perfect. Within months, Groom Lake became the training area for the U-2 spy plane, one of the most effective U.S. spy planes ever launched.

Though it quickly became a key part of U.S. defense activities, Area 51 was cleared of employees in 1957 after a nuclear bomb, the Hood bomb, was detonated in a test nearby. The site was saturated with deadly, **radioactive** plutonium. The bomb was six times more powerful than those dropped on Hiroshima and Nagasaki, Japan, in 1945. It is still the largest nuclear bomb ever detonated over the continental United States. Area 51 remained closed and deserted until 1960. That's when design began on a plane invisible to radar that would fly higher and faster than the U-2. The Area 51 runway was extended to nearly 6 miles (9.7 km) in length. The restricted airspace above it was expanded

U-2 SPY PLANE

15

THE COLD WAR

At the end of World War II (1939–45), the former Allied powers—the United States, Great Britain, and the Soviet Union—disagreed on how to rebuild Europe. The Soviet Union wanted to control its neighbors and spread communism. The United States and Great Britain wanted to establish capitalist, democratic states. All had seen the destructive power of the world's first atomic bomb, dropped by the United States over Japan in 1945. They understood the dangerous potential of that technology. But the nations were also at odds. So, they resorted to a new way of fighting: the Cold War. It was a conflict in which, for nearly 50 years, the United States and the Soviet Union built and tested nuclear weapons and threatened to use them. The Cold War turned spying into an international industry. That led directly to the development of Area 51 as a test site for breakthrough aircraft. Without the need for Cold War secrecy, Area 51 may never have existed.

from 50 square miles (129 sq km) to 440 square miles (1,140 sq km). The growth allowed for development of the Archangel 12 (A-12); the SR-71 Blackbird, which flew in the 1990s Persian Gulf War; and the F-117 Nighthawk, a key player in the Persian Gulf as well as in the War on Terror.

Such engineering has made Area 51 a busy place, although it is still remote and inhospitable. It is windy and dusty. Temperatures can fluctuate from 100 degrees Fahrenheit (38 degrees Celsius) on summer days to 0 °F (-18 °C) on winter nights. Daily temperature swings of 40 degrees are considered normal. Yet the U.S. Air Force, CIA, and aircraft manufacturer Lockheed ultimately installed barracks, dining halls, and other amenities for hundreds of workers. These workers were flown to Area 51 weekly from Las Vegas on commercial jets with the windows covered. On the ground, they were often shuttled from place to place on buses, also with windows blacked out.

It wasn't until 1978 that the nearby town of Rachel, Nevada, was established. The community of about 100 people sat along Route 375 about 25 miles (40 km) outside the east gate of Area 51. Rachel was as close as anyone without high-level **security clearance** or a sturdy vehicle could get to Area 51. Over time, the town attracted a steady stream of curious people. They wanted to know about secret aircraft, lights in the night sky, **sonic booms**, and what seemed to be a concentration of UFOs.

NOTHING TO SEE HERE?

17

A MANUFACTURED MYSTERY

Area 51 has always placed a premium on secrecy. As a project developed in part by the CIA, the lead U.S. intelligence-gathering agency, the site's concealment was of top importance. The remote location in the desert aided that effort, but the secrecy went much farther. Employees were often not told what their work was about or how it related to work others were doing. In the 1980s, employees had to sign pledges. They agreed they would not discuss their work with anybody, under penalty of 10 years in prison or a $10,000 fine. As a result, the work at Area 51 became known as "black projects." The cost and purpose was concealed even from Congress. (It's been reported that the Area 51 budget is about $1 billion per year.) When an A-12 from Area 51 crashed in Utah in 1963 and a vacationing family came upon the wreckage, CIA officials who had pursued the aircraft took the film from the family's camera and paid them off in cash. Similarly, in 1962, when a Greyhound bus

A FAKE ALIEN SPACECRAFT

scraped against a trailer carrying parts of an A-12 to Area 51, officials quietly paid $5,000 to cover damages to the bus to prevent an insurance claim.

When some workers developed diseases they believed were caused by the burning of toxic materials at Area 51 (not even the trash was allowed to be carried out, so everything was destroyed on site), they went to court in 1994 to discover the truth. However, the U.S. government sealed all records related to the case, even those of the workers' lawyer, preventing the public from seeing them. President Bill Clinton then exempted Area 51 from Environmental Protection Agency requirements that inventories of hazardous waste be made public. In 1998, the courts ruled that the trial could not continue, since the government would not provide key information.

OPPOSITE: Bomb- and missile-testing activities were common near Area 51 in the 1950s.

But the case cracked the walls of secrecy around Area 51. More than 40 years after it began testing the U-2 there, the U.S. government finally acknowledged that it had "an operating location near Groom Lake." But that was all.

The government may have surrounded Area 51 with secrecy to prevent other nations from learning about U.S. military technology. But the secrecy had a strange effect on the United States itself. In 1947, shortly after the end of World War II, when international relations were tense and uncertain, a mysterious aircraft crashed in the desert outside Roswell, New Mexico. It was first described by the

ROSWELL

The modern UFO era can be traced to the World War II era, when extensive air combat brought new awareness of the dangers the skies could bring. In 1947, thousands of people across the United States reported seeing "flying saucers" in the sky. One incident became central to the myth of alien contact: the announcement by an officer at Roswell Army Air Field in New Mexico that they had recovered the debris of a crashed flying saucer. The next day, officials announced that the "ship" was just a weather balloon—but UFOlogists refused to accept that explanation. Roswell's reputation also involved Area 51, situated nearly 1,000 miles (1,609 km) west. According to the story, whatever crashed near Roswell, including live alien crew members, was first taken to Wright-Patterson Air Force base in Ohio. Then it was removed to Area 51 for further research. The stories were kept alive by fringe publications such as *Fate Magazine*. And they have continued to be part of American popular culture through movies and TV shows such as *Close Encounters of the Third Kind* and *The X-Files*.

OPPOSITE: Military officials examine supposed alien spacecraft remains from New Mexico in 1947.

U.S. Army as a flying saucer—an account that was amended within a day. The occurrence was one of a wave of UFO reports. And these reports gave rise to decades of speculation about the military hiding extraterrestrial secrets. They inspired many fictional accounts of aliens in film, television, and books.

According to a CIA report released in 1997, the agency had investigated nearly 1,000 UFO reports by 1951, often interviewing citizen-witnesses but swearing them to secrecy. Faced with a public that seemed convinced that UFOs had come from elsewhere in the universe, guided by intelligent beings using sophisticated technology, the U.S. government was in a delicate spot. If aliens really had landed, could the government tell the public? Wouldn't people begin to doubt the government's defense systems? Would citizens panic? Would they think an invasion from outer space was happening? If any extraterrestrials had survived, where were they? And why were they here? Despite the secrecy, or maybe because of it, an undercurrent of fringe belief began to develop. It included stories that aliens were here to abduct humans, perhaps to perform medical experiments or simply to make friends. Maybe the aliens were up to something more sinister.

One idea emerged among conspiracy theorists that the U.S. government and the visitors had struck a deal: The aliens would teach the military how to build aircraft like theirs—extremely fast, capable of hovering and darting from side to side, and able to accelerate with

OPPOSITE: In 1939, mistaking a fictional radiodrama for news, many Americans were convinced an alien invasion was underway.

unimaginable quickness. If the government was engaged in developing sophisticated aircraft at Area 51, it stood to reason (to some) that aliens were also being held there. That seemed to explain the secrecy.

U.S. citizens had been carried away by UFO dramas before. In 1939, nationwide hysteria erupted when listeners mistook the broadcast of the science-fiction radiodrama *War of the Worlds* for a real space invasion. In 1947, there was a nationwide wave of "flying saucers" sightings. In the early 1960s, the CIA was concerned that similar **hoaxes** could divert the nation's air defense system so thoroughly that the United States would be vulnerable to a real enemy, such as the Soviet Union. For a while, the Air Force cooperated with UFOlogists. But author Annie Jacobsen, in her book *Area 51: An Uncensored History of America's Top Secret Military Base*, asserts that there was hidden reason. Such teamwork simply allowed the CIA to investigate the people who had collected vast amounts of information about UFOs and find out what they knew.

AN ALIEN ILLUSTRATION FROM WAR OF THE WORLDS

A series of U.S. government commissions through the 1950s and '60s determined that UFOs were not real. Public interest died down, though not completely. Meanwhile, Area 51's secret expansion continued well into the 1980s. Some historians argue that the government was willing to allow UFOs to be the subject of public controversy for good reason: Such speculations diverted attention from the very real, top secret aeronautical breakthroughs at Area 51. But outside the base, questions remained. What were those hovering, darting, intensely bright lights people kept seeing above Area 51?

A MANUFACTURED MYSTERY

25

LITTLE GRAY ALIENS

In 1989, the cloak of secrecy on Area 51 was torn away. A man named Bob Lazar gave a series of interviews to a Las Vegas TV station. He detailed what he said was his work on the captured alien technology held at the base. Lazar is a deeply controversial figure, surrounded by legends, many of his own making. For instance, he has claimed to have earned master's degrees in both electronic technology from the California Institute of Technology and physics from the Massachusetts Institute of Technology. However, neither college has record of his attendance. Despite the discrepancy, in 1989, his story met a wide audience and brought significant attention to Area 51.

Lazar's story is that after a news article was published about a jet-powered car Lazar had designed himself, he was contacted by physicist Edward Teller, known as the "Father of the Hydrogen Bomb." Teller invited Lazar to work on a project in Nevada involving aircraft. Lazar signed an oath swearing he'd never reveal what he was working on

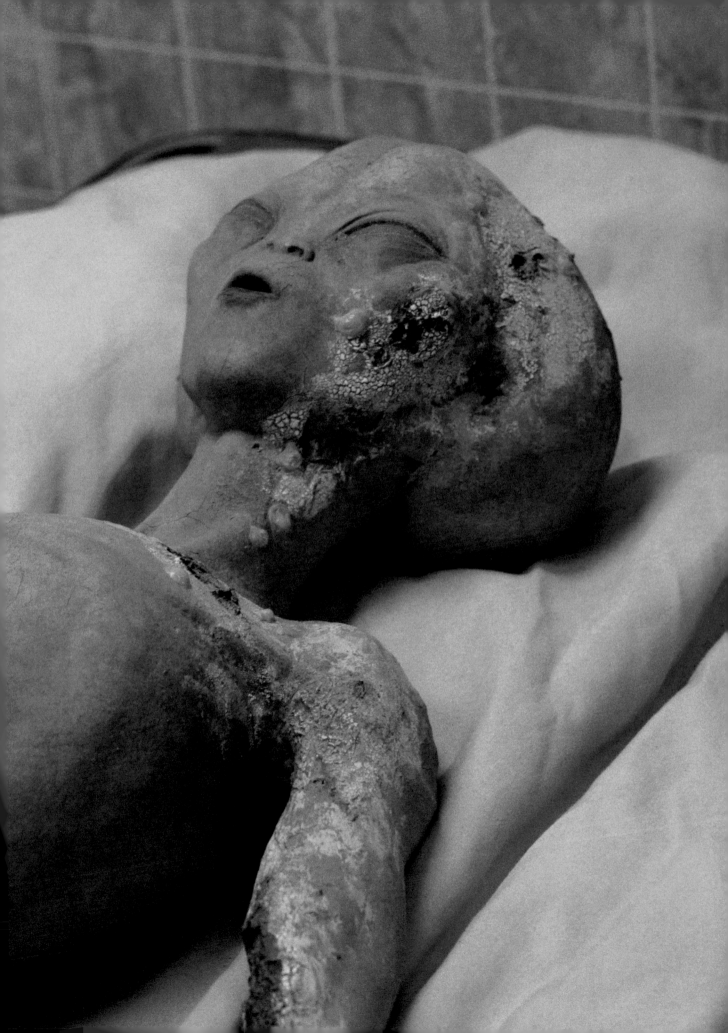

and agreed to have his phone tapped and his car and home searched without warning. He reported to the Las Vegas airport, was flown to a base north of the city, and was taken in a bus with blacked-out windows to a secret facility. There, in a hangar, he saw a large, disk-shaped craft with tiny seats. He was taken to a room, handed a stack of material to study, and left alone. When his escort closed the door, Lazar saw a poster on the back of the door. It showed a picture of a dry lakebed with a saucerlike craft and the words "They're here."

OPPOSITE: An alien recreation on display in a Roswell, New Mexico, museum

Over time, Lazar determined the vehicles in the hangar had been fueled by **Element** 115. Lazar theorized that the substance could have unique gravitational properties as it decayed, allowing aircraft to travel great distances. He also claimed to have read **autopsy** reports of bodies that had been in the aircraft. The reports referred to "the kids" and described them as short and hairless, with gray skin, large heads, and almond-shaped eyes. Lazar even glimpsed a living one through the window of a room as he was being ushered past. He studied documents stating that the spacecraft had come from Zeta Reticuli, a **binary** star system 200 trillion miles (322 trillion km) away. Several years before, a husband and wife who claimed they'd been abducted by aliens had said their abductors had come from Zeta Reticuli.

Lazar told interviewers that what had already been learned at Area 51 needed the involvement of more scientists, not secrecy. "Just the concept

LITTLE GRAY ALIENS

29

that there's definite proof, and we can even have articles from another world, another system . . . you can't just not tell everyone," Lazar said.

But, Lazar said, when he was caught with several friends trying to get a closer look at what he'd told them were test flights of disks at Area 51, he was fired. A short time later, he gave his interview on Las Vegas television in a way that concealed his identity. He claimed later that he was run off the highway and shot at in his car by people he believed were trying to guard Area 51's secrecy. That led him to reveal his identity as a way of protecting himself. He quickly became a folk hero to UFOlogists, and for a while, he was cohost of a Las Vegas radio show. However, his story was undermined when the universities he claimed to have attended reported they had no records of him. Lazar said the U.S. government had stolen the evidence and destroyed his birth certificate, but the damage was done.

Like Lazar, Glenn Campbell called himself a "lobbyist for openness." Campbell, who had made some money designing a computer program for banks, moved from Boston to Rachel, Nevada, in 1993, after the Air Force had expanded the restricted area surrounding Area 51. Working in a bar-restaurant in the desert outpost and calling himself "Psychospy," Campbell published his own document called *The Area 51 Viewer's Guide.* He advised the growing number of visitors on their rights and the proper responses if confronted by security agents when venturing close to Area 51. He also posted a regular online newsletter called "The Groom Lake Desert Rat," a wide-ranging compendium of news, science, speculation, policy,

SAUCERS: KEEP LEFT

Nevada Route 375 carries traffic through nearly 100 miles (161 km) of desert from Ash Springs to Warm Springs. Officially designated as the Extraterrestrial Highway, the road runs within about 25 miles (40 km) of Area 51, closer than any other major thoroughfare. The designation accompanied the promotion of the 1996 20th Century Fox film *Independence Day*, in which Area 51 is a key location. When the Nevada legislature nixed the highway name change, Governor Bob Miller got the state transportation board to authorize it anyway. The 1996 dedication at the Little A-Le-Inn in Rachel, Nevada, was attended by numerous movie stars. There was even a person claiming to represent the "intergalactic tourism association." The highway, still one of the least-traveled roads in Nevada, is now posted with green signs showing pictures of flying saucers. But even though it passes through wide-open, lonely country, drivers still have to watch how fast they're going. The speed limit is Warp 7.

ALIEN ABDUCTION WARNING SIGN

and politics. Campbell called the trailer he moved into the "Area 51 Research Center." He explored and marked a route to an overlook just outside Area 51 that he named "Freedom Ridge." In 1994, he took a Nevada state legislator up Freedom Ridge. The purpose was to show him how the activity and development at Area 51 proved the U.S. Air Force hadn't been paying enough property taxes to surrounding Lincoln County. Campbell also published the radio frequencies that the Area 51 security guards used, as well as arrival and departure times for the planes carrying workers from and to Las Vegas.

Campbell was in some ways the opposite of Lazar. He didn't believe in aliens. His *Viewer's Guide* warns people that the most dangerous creatures they might encounter are not aliens or security patrols but cows. In an interview with author David Darlington for his book *Area 51: The Dreamland Chronicles,* Campbell said the community of UFO followers "is full of nuts and ridiculous folklore." He said that UFO sightings simply are examples of people's imaginations at work. "When people look at a light in the sky, what they see indicates something about what's inside of them," he said. "I'm not into UFOs," he continued. "I'm into humanity and philosophy."

Lazar and Campbell were part of an eccentric band of Area 51 monitors who occasionally put the town of Rachel in the national news. Others include Peter Merlin and Joerg Arnu, who run

LITTLE GRAY ALIENS

33

Dreamland Resort, an informational website that keeps track of events at Area 51. The more serious of these monitors focus on speculations about aircraft testing. But they wouldn't have caught the public eye in such a way without the UFOs and extraterrestrials. Underlying Area 51's mysteriousness is the notion that it is the place where the remains of the 1947 Roswell crash are being kept, examined, and perhaps duplicated. That possibility has sparked the imaginations not only of UFOlogists but also of the Nevada tourism industry, Hollywood, and other generators of American popular culture. Aliens make a good story.

Several elements of Lazar's story—such as Zeta Reticuli and Element 115—were key features of the TV series *Seven Days*, which dealt with a time-traveling spacecraft developed from the Roswell remains. The 1996 action film *Independence Day* used Area 51 as the place where the president was taken to hide from attacking aliens and where the Roswell remains were used to repel the attack and ultimately save the world. A 2005 video game, *Area 51*, is built on the notion of aliens trading their technological know-how for human test subjects. The subjects would provide the aliens with a virus to use in a war in their home world. And some who argue that the 1969 Apollo moon landing was a hoax say it was all filmed at Area 51.

The TV series *The X-Files*, which involved a long-running plotline about a conspiracy to hide evidence of extraterrestrial contact, set one

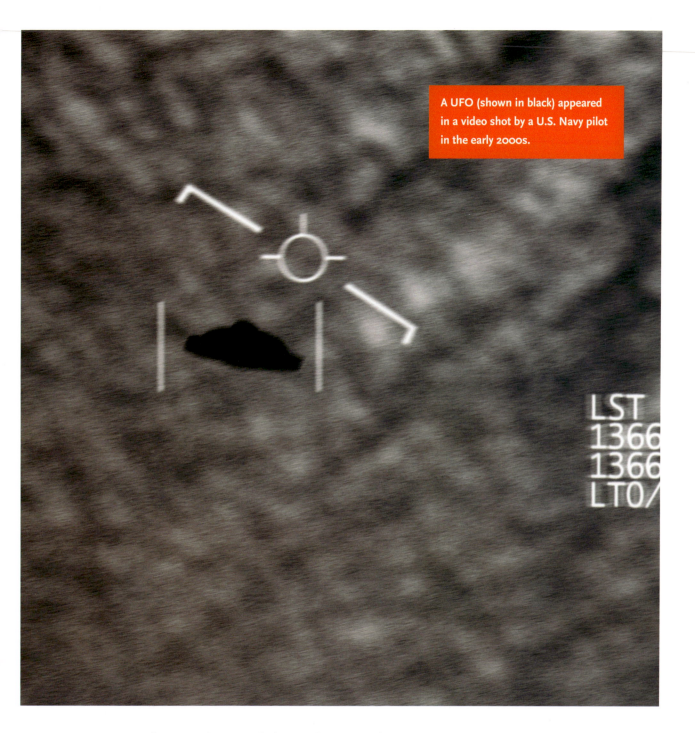

A UFO (shown in black) appeared in a video shot by a U.S. Navy pilot in the early 2000s.

of its episodes in Rachel, Nevada. In real life, Rachel has styled itself as "The UFO Capital of the World." It has also become a draw for **geocachers**, thanks to the 1,500 geocaches placed along Route 375, the "Extraterrestrial Highway," in 2011.

WATCH THE SKIES

Some of the cloud of mystery around Area 51 has evaporated in recent years. Details of the U-2 project were **declassified** in 1998. They allowed it to be known—more than 40 years after the fact—that pilot Ray Goudey had been the first man to fly a plane higher than 65,000 feet (19,812 meters). In 2007, decades after workers at Area 51 would hustle the A-12 into a hangar to keep it from being viewed by satellites, the CIA displayed an A-12 in front of its Langley, Virginia, headquarters. The showing was part of the agency's 60th anniversary celebration. The public was allowed to stroll by the titanium-skinned aircraft that could fly up to an altitude of 90,000 feet (27,432 m) at 3 times the speed of sound. The A-12 has rarely been seen in flight, although it is believed that many reported UFO sightings have been extremely fast and highly reflective A-12s.

OPPOSITE: Despite the U.S. military's revelations, many mysteries, especially involving alien visitors, still exist.

OPPOSITE: UFOs spotted over Salem, Massachusetts, in 1952 may have actually been classified military aircraft.

In the early days of stealth technology, the SR-71 Blackbird was groundbreaking. Such aircraft used angled surfaces and materials that absorbed radar beams. On radar, the 107-foot-long (33-m) Blackbird, with a wingspan of nearly 58 feet (18 m), appeared to have an area of 108 square feet (10 sq m). Thirty-two SR-71s were built. Most had long careers, flying from 1964 to 1998.

The F-117 Nighthawk (active from 1981 to 2008) represented a vast improvement in radar-evasion technology. Although it was 66 feet (20 m) long with a wingspan of 43 feet (13 m), the bat-shaped aircraft appeared on radar to be the same size as a ball bearing! Area 51 might have needed secrecy to operate in its first three decades, but now it was producing secrecy itself, in a way.

Drone technology—flying aircraft by remote control—was first used in World War II. It did not meet with great success then, but the CIA pursued the idea and produced the Predator drone in the 1990s for **reconnaissance** purposes. By 2000, concerned about the activities of al Qaeda terrorist Osama bin Laden, the CIA outfitted the Predator with Hellfire missiles, and, for training, built a mockup of bin Laden's compound in Afghanistan on the edge of Area 51. In 2012, according to reports, Predators flying in the Middle East were being operated by "pilots" at computers just outside Area 51.

A year later, in August 2013, the U.S. government officially acknowledged the existence of Area 51 by declassifying a 1992 CIA report. Some believed the move indicated the government was

becoming less secretive. Others wondered if the news was meant to prepare the public for the truth about alien activities.

Declassification also gave a dramatic twist to Area 51's long-simmering flying saucer tales. In her 2011 book, Annie Jacobsen reports that the disks that crashed at Roswell in 1947 were most definitely not from another planet. She says they were from the Soviet Union. **Cyrillic** writing inside the craft confirmed that fact, she says.

According to Jacobsen, the Soviets had exploited disk-flight technology developed by German Nazis. But her book makes an even more dramatic assertion. Quoting an unnamed engineer who worked on the remains of the crash, Jacobsen writes that the creatures in the craft were human children. Their large heads and strange eyes were, in fact, examples of human experimentation by Nazis during and after World War II, under an agreement between the Nazis and Soviet dictator Joseph Stalin. Stalin, the engineer was told, believed that by sending the small aviators in a disk to crash in the United States, he could cause a panic. Area 51 employees quoted elsewhere in the book said after it was published that they were unaware of any such things happening at Area 51 and were shocked to read about them.

Even after declassification, the U.S. government has preferred not to say anything about Area 51. In recent years, though, several whistleblowers have come forward with surprising tales of UFO contact. The most striking came from U.S. Navy pilots and Pentagon officials. Their credentials would seem to make them a reliable source of information. By 2023, the government had collected more than 500 reports of "unidentified anomalous phenomena." That new term, shortened as "UAP," is now considered the official term for mysterious sky sightings, rather than "UFOs." The broader term includes the possibility that the sightings might be things such as weather patterns or optical illusions instead of "flying objects."

In 2017, *The New York Times* reported on several videos showing incidents between UFOs and the U.S. military. In one shot in 2004, Navy pilot and commander David Fravor encounters a mysterious white oval object. Apparently an aircraft, it moved unlike any known plane. It dived 60,000 feet (18,288 m) at astonishing speed and accelerated so fast that it seemed to fly 60 miles (97 km) away in less than a minute—far faster than the top speed of Fravor's state-of-the-art F/A-18F Super Hornet jet.

Fravor testified to Congress in 2023 that he believed what he saw was some form of alien technology. Major David Grusch, a retired Pentagon official who once worked for the agency's UAP Task Force,

also testified that he believed the U.S. government had been concealing knowledge of extraterrestrial visits to Earth since the 1930s. He believed that a secret military program had been retrieving crashed alien spacecraft, and even non-human "biologics," and attempting to reverse-engineer the technology. However, he didn't say where the activities were allegedly taking place. The Pentagon denied Grusch's claims.

What could these things be? On June 25, 2021, the Pentagon released a nine-page document titled "Preliminary Assessment: Unidentified Aerial Phenomena." It rounded up the results of the investigations of 144 incidents of UAP sightings by U.S. armed forces. Mostly inconclusive, it was able to give a definite answer to only one of the 144 UAPs, which it said was a balloon. As for the others, the report gave possible explanations. They included birds, weather-related things such as ice crystals or clouds, and airborne human-made trash. Some UAPs might have been U.S. military aircraft or drones that are still classified and, therefore, could not be officially explained. Still others might have been technology used by foreign nations such as Russia or China. In that case, the Pentagon might not yet know all the answers and might not be able to talk about it even if it did, for reasons of national security. The document also admitted that there was no explanation at all for many sightings because of limited information or a need for further study.

Science writer Mick West, a vocal **skeptic** of UFO claims, notes that it is difficult to gauge the truth of a sighting based on a few seconds of camera footage taken by a jet flying at very high speeds. He told *New York*

Magazine in 2023, "You can't rule out aliens, obviously, but you need to recognize that they're the least likely of the possible explanations."

Ohio State University professor Christopher McKnight Nichols, an expert in the history of U.S. national security, told the *Houston Chronicle* in 2023 that many UFO sightings in the Area 51 region "match almost exactly with dates and times of flights of then-classified experimental aircraft. And we know that more recently classified drone and other aerial surveillance and military technologies have been tested at the site. In the end, there is no reason to think that anything other than earthly technologies have been behind the strange sights and sounds at Area 51." Although it's no longer classified, Area 51's remoteness still makes it valuable for secret projects. The base is still closed to the public and most military air traffic. But that very secrecy also allows the rumors and speculations about aliens to thrive.

In 2022, the Pentagon opened the All-Domain Anomaly Resolution Office (AARO). It was a task group whose purpose was to investigate and analyze UAP reports. Many of these sightings had been sent in by military pilots. At least some occurred near areas of sensitive or classified national-security status.

Sean Kirkpatrick, a physics professor and founding director of AARO, told the magazine *Scientific American* in 2023 that his office's official report would show that most UAP sightings had nothing to do with aliens. "Some are misrepresentations, and some derive from pure, unsupported beliefs," he said. The report was released in 2024, and it stated there was no evidence that any UAP sighting "represented extraterrestrial technology."

U.S. government officials may or may not think these sightings are aliens, but they still have to investigate them, because it's not yet proven what they actually are. If they're optical illusions or fakes, they can be ignored. If they're evidence of foreign spies, that might require a diplomatic

A GOOD GUESS

The U.S. Air Force designed its F-117 Nighthawk to avoid radar detection, but a plastic toy model turned out to be anything but invisible to consumers. A designer for Testor Corporation, John Andrews, used publicly available information—filling in gaps with his own understanding of military aircraft—to design a model of the stealth fighter he guessed the Air Force was building at Area 51 in the early 1980s. Testor unveiled its F-19 Stealth Fighter model in 1986. Although, or perhaps because, the Air Force refused to acknowledge the plane existed, Testor soon sold more than 700,000 of the models, making it the most popular aircraft model ever. Once the F-117 was publicly revealed two years later, people realized that the model was very different from the real thing. Still, the popularity of the model and the refusal by the Air Force to acknowledge anything about the real plane prompted hearings to be held in Congress, an example of how secrecy can work against itself. Andrews regarded models as teaching tools, and although he was an Army veteran, he was also critical of the government for concealing information from its own citizens.

or military response. But until people know what's actually happening, they won't know what to do. There are legitimate national security reasons for secrecy about government research into high-tech planes, drones, and rocketry. But it comes with a side effect: Secrecy also gives conspiracy theories and other fringe beliefs a place to grow. And what if the sightings really are aliens? Then maybe humans should say hello.

These days, the town of Rachel, Nevada, is quieter than it used to be. After the Air Force expanded the secure zone around Area 51 in 1995 to include Freedom Ridge, Glenn Campbell moved away. His Area 51 Research Center closed in 2001, and Campbell died in 2021. In 2023, the only operating businesses in Rachel included a gas station, the Dreamland Resort website, and the Little A-le-Inn, home of the "Alien Burger."

In 2019, about 3,000 people showed up to an event called Storm Area 51, after an Internet meme went viral. Some camped near the base, though none were allowed inside. The town was unhappy with the massive influx of visitors. Even the town's official website called the event "rather unremarkable." It's unlikely to be repeated. Rachel, like Area 51 itself, prefers quiet. But no matter how many documents get declassified or how many reports of UFOs are debunked, Area 51 will continue to draw people seeking contact with other worlds and eager to probe the mysteries that surround it.

45

FIELD NOTES

aeronautics—the study or practice of aircraft navigation

autopsy—an examination of a dead body to determine the cause of death

binary—having two parts

budget—the amount of money required to operate a household, office, government, or other enterprise

conspiracy—a secret plan, involving several or many participants, to accomplish something unlawful or harmful

Cyrillic—an alphabet derived from the Greek alphabet and used for Slavic languages, including Russian

declassified—opened to the public; no longer secret

element—a substance that cannot be broken down into simpler components

extraterrestrial—something that originates beyond the Earth; alien

geocacher—a person who, for recreation, finds items hidden in the landscape by using a global positioning device

hoax—a humorous or harmful deception; trick

intelligence—information having military, political, or other strategic value

irony—the occurrence of the opposite of what might be expected

radioactive—emitting ionizing radiation or particles

reconnaissance—a search for useful military information

security clearance—permission to enter guarded places or read certain secret material

skeptic—a person who doubts or questions a claim

sonic boom—an explosive sound made by the compression of sound waves as an object moves at the speed of sound

SELECTED BIBLIOGRAPHY

Darlington, David. *Area 51: The Dreamland Chronicles*. New York: H. Holt, 1997.

Jacobsen, Annie. *Area 51: An Uncensored History of America's Top Secret Military Base*. New York: Little, Brown and Co., 2011.

Merlin, Peter W. *Dreamland: The Secret History of Area 51*. Atglen, Pa.: Schiffer Publishing, 2023.

Patton, Phil. *Dreamland: Travels Inside the Secret World of Roswell and Area 51*. New York: Villard, 1998.

Rich, Ben R., and Leo Janos. *Skunk Works: A Personal Memoir of My Years at Lockheed*. Boston: Little, Brown, 1994.

Wright, Susan. *UFO Headquarters: Investigations on Current Exraterrestrial Activity*. New York: St. Martin's Press, 1998.

Yenne, Bill. *Area 51 Black Jets*. Minneapolis: Zenith Press, 2014.

WEBSITES

Dreamland Resort
https://www.dreamlandresort.com
Read news and history about Area 51.

Rachel, Nevada
https://www.rachel-nevada.com
Explore the official website of the capital of the Extraterrestrial Highway.

INDEX

airplanes
    Archangel 12 (A-12), 17, 18, 21
    F-117 Nighthawk, 17, 38, 41, 43
    SR-71 Blackbird, 17, 38
    U-2, 12, 14, 15, 21, 37
aliens, 9, 19, 22, 23, 24, 27, 29, 33, 34, 37, 39, 40, 41, 42
All-Domain Anomaly Resolution Office (AARO), 42
Andrews, John, 43
Area 51 (video game), 34
Arnu, Joerg, 34
bin Laden, Osama, 38
Bissell, Richard, 14
budget, 18
Campbell, Glenn, 30, 33, 45
Central Intelligence Agency (CIA), 14, 17, 18, 23, 24, 37, 38
Clinton, Bill, 21
Cold War, 10, 16
Darlington, David, 33
declassification, 37, 38, 39, 40
Dreamland Resort website, 34, 45
Eisenhower, Dwight D., 14
Element 115, 29, 34
employees, 9, 10, 15, 17, 18, 30, 40
Extraterrestrial Highway. *See* Nevada Route 375
F-19 Stealth Fighter (toy), 43
Fravor, David, 40
Freedom Ridge, 33, 45
Goudey, Ray, 37
Groom Lake, 13, 14, 21, 30
Grusch, David, 40–41
Hood bomb, 15
Jacobsen, Annie, 24, 39
Johnson, Lyndon, 12, 13
Kirkpatrick, Sean, 42
Las Vegas, Nevada, 9, 13, 17, 29, 30, 33
Lazar, Bob, 27, 29–30, 33, 34
location, 9, 12–13, 14, 18
Lockheed, 17
Merlin, Peter, 13, 34

Miller, Bob, 32
movies and TV, 9, 22, 23, 32, 34, 35
names, 9, 13–14
Nazis, 39
Nevada National Security Site, 13
Nevada Route 375, 17, 32, 35
Nevada Test and Training Range (NTTR), 13, 14
Nichols, Christopher McKnight, 42
Pentagon, 40, 41, 42
Predator drones, 38
Rachel, Nevada, 17, 30, 32, 33, 35, 45
Roswell, New Mexico, 21, 22, 23, 29, 34, 39
security, Area 51, 13, 17, 18, 21, 29, 30, 33
sightings
    Lazar's aircraft project, 27, 29–30, 34
    military, 9, 35, 40, 41, 42
    Roswell saucer crash, 21, 22, 23, 34, 39
size, 13, 15, 17
Soviet Union, 10, 14, 16, 24, 39
Stalin, Joseph, 39
Storm Area 51, 45
Teller, Edward, 27
temperatures, 17
UAPs, 40, 41, 42
UFOs, 10, 17, 22, 23, 24, 25, 30, 33, 34, 35, 37, 38, 40, 41, 42, 45
U.S. Air Force, 17, 24, 30, 33, 43, 45
U.S. Navy, 35, 40
War of the Worlds, 24
West, Mick, 41–42
World War II, 16, 21, 22, 38, 39
Zeta Reticuli, 29, 30, 34

ENDURING MYSTERIES — AREA 51

48